loving myself

when i love you more
than i love myself
i am really loving you less

loving myself less than you
i make it harder
for you to love me

your love for me
is so very dependent
on the love i have for myself

and my love for you
will be stronger
if you love yourself the way you love me

—Ulrich Schaffer

Love Yourself

Walter Trobisch

Self-Acceptance & Depression

InterVarsity Press
Downers Grove
Illinois 60515

InterVarsity Press is the book-publishing division of Inter-Varsity Christian Fellowship, a student movement active on campus at hundreds of universities, colleges and schools of nursing. For information about local and regional activities, write IVCF, 233 Langdon St., Madison, WI 53703.

Distributed in Canada through InterVarsity Press, 1875 Leslie St., Unit 10, Don Mills, Ontario M3B 2M5, Canada.

Unless otherwise noted, biblical quotations are from the Revised Standard Version, copyrighted 1946, 1952, © 1971, 1973.

ISBN 0-87784-576-X
Library of Congress Catalog Card Number: 75-44639

Printed in the United States of America

The poem "Loving Myself" by Ulrich Schaffer is reprinted by permission of Harper and Row, Publishers, from Love Reaches Out, Copyright © 1976 by Ulrich Schaffer.

19	18	17	16	15	14	13
90	89	88	87	86	85	

1 Do I Love Myself?

The girl entered our hotel room. It was the day after my wife and I had given a lecture at one of the universities in northern Europe. The hotel room was the only place we had for counseling.

She was a beautiful Scandinavian girl. Long blond hair fell over her shoulders. Gracefully she sat down in the armchair offered to her and looked at us with deep and vivid blue eyes. Her long arms allowed her to fold her hands over her knees. We noticed her fine, slender, fingers, revealing a very tender, precious personality.

"I am a beautiful girl." As we discussed her problems, we came back again and again to one basic issue which seemed to be the root of all the others. It was the problem which we had least expected when she entered the room: She could not love herself. In fact, she hated herself to such a degree that she was only one step away from putting an end to her life.

To point out to her the apparent gifts she had—her success as a student, the favorable impression she had made upon us by her outward appearance—seemed to be of no avail. She refused to acknowledge anything good about herself. She was afraid that any self-appreciation she might express would mean giving in to the temptation of pride, and to be proud meant to be rejected by God. She had grown up in a tight-laced religious family and had learned that self-depreciation was Christian and self-rejection the only way to find acceptance by God.

We asked her to stand up and take a look in the mirror. She turned her head away. With gentle force I held her head so that she had to look into her own eyes. She cringed as if she were experiencing physical pain.

It took a long time before she was able to whisper, though unconvinced, the sentence I asked her to repeat, "I am a beautiful girl."

Nobody loves himself. It is an established fact that nobody is born with the ability to love himself.

The German psychotherapist Dr. Guido Groeger summarizes the findings of modern psychology by saying, *The opinion seems to be widespread that everyone loves himself and that all that is necessary would be to constantly remind people to love others.*

It is up to the theologian to decide how to interpret the word of the Lord, "Love your neighbor as yourself"—

whether as a commandment and a statement or as a double commandment.

In any case the psychologist has to underline the fact that there is in man no inborn self-love. Self-love is either acquired or it is non-existent. The one who does not acquire it or who acquires it insufficiently either is not able to love others at all or to love them only insufficiently. The same would be true for such a person also in his relationship to God.

It is true that the foundation for this ability to accept oneself is laid in early childhood. But it is also true that an adult needs the assurance of being affirmed and accepted sometimes to a greater and sometimes to a lesser degree, depending upon the different situations of his life.

Because this affirmation is often withheld—especially in Christian circles—a type of Christian is created who loves out of duty and who in this way tortures not only others, but also himself.

Often the choice of a profession is motivated by such a deficiency of love. One hopes to satisfy one's own needs by satisfying the needs of others. But this is a miscalculation. [1]

On the other hand the Catholic philosopher, Romano Guardini in his essay, "The Acceptance of Oneself," writes, "The act of self-acceptance is the root of all things. I must agree to be the person who I am. Agree to have the qualifications which I have. Agree to live within the limitations set for me. . . . The clarity and the courageousness of this acceptance is the foundation of all existence."

If both statements are true, if on the one hand self-acceptance is the foundation of all existence and if on the other hand nobody is born with the ability to accept and love oneself, we face a real challenge. A tremendous task is laid before us, and each one has to ask himself—

Have I accepted myself fully and completely?

With my gifts? With my limits? With my dangers?

Have I accepted my lot? My gender? My sexuality? My age?

Do I say yes to my marriage? To my children? To my parents? To my being single?

Do I say yes to my economic situation? To my state of health? To the way I look?

In short, do I love myself?

In our day the words love and acceptance have become interchangeable, and thus far I have used them synonymously, for I believe that this is helpful. Since the word *love* is often abused and has become trite and meaningless, I have used the word *acceptance* to prevent us from viewing love as merely romantic, sentimental or sexual. To love means to accept the other as he really is.

Precisely this was one of the problems of our student visitor in that hotel room. She could not get along with anyone, neither with her fellow students, nor with her professors, nor with her neighbors, nor with her own family. She was full of hostility and criticism.

When we asked her for an explanation she blamed it all on herself. She said that she loved herself too much, thought only of herself and called herself an egoist. For this reason she could not accept others and really love them.

We had to contradict her. We claimed that just the opposite was true. It was difficult for her to love others because she did not love herself enough. It is impossible for us to accept the other one as he is if we have not accepted ourselves as we are.

Love yourself. This sheds a new light on the command which Jesus emphasized as ranking in importance next to loving God: "You shall love your neighbor as yourself" (Mt. 22:39, Mk. 12:31, Lk. 10:27).

In the Bible we first find this command in Leviticus 19:18. Besides the verses mentioned above, this command is found in three other crucial places in the New Testament, each of which succinctly summarizes the passage in which it is found. Galatians 5:14 summarizes the "whole law" in one word, "You shall love your neighbor as yourself." Likewise James 2:8 gives this command as a fulfillment of the "royal law," and Romans 13:9 gives it as the summation of "all the commandments." The command to love your neighbor is never given without the command to love yourself.

Usually it is assumed that everyone loves himself. Everyone is an egoist. And we are taught that this is wrong; instead of loving ourselves, we should love our neighbor. However, this is not what the verses state. They do not say, "Love your neighbor *instead* of yourself," but "Love your neighbor *as* yourself." Self-love is thus the prerequisite and criterion for our conduct toward our neighbor. It is the measuring stick for loving others which Jesus gives us.[3]

We find that the Bible confirms what modern psychology has recently discovered: Without self-love there can be no love for others. Jesus equates these two loves, and binds them together, making them inseparable.

The question now is how Jesus could assume that in his listeners this self-love, which Dr. Groeger says must be acquired, is naturally present. Part of the answer may lie in the fact that the people of Jesus' time were more composed and less neurotic than modern man. They found it easier to acquire self-acceptance and to like themselves. Therefore, Jesus could assume that his hearers had learned to accept themselves to a degree people today have yet to learn. What was presumed as a natural characteristic in their time is something which is difficult for modern man to acquire.

Could it be that the difficulty in loving ourselves is also one of the negative side-effects of our so-called civilization?

When I write this I have to think of many of my African friends. It seems so much easier for them to accept themselves than for us Westerners. I am reminded of one of my best friends, an African man who is rather short. A well-meaning person once suggested to him that he wear shoes with higher heels in order to appear taller.

This was almost an offense to my friend. Hadn't God made him short? Why should he seek to change what God had created? He had accepted himself as he was and loved himself with his height. I am sure this complete self-acceptance is one of the reasons that he can be such a good friend to me.

In the passage describing the friendship between David and Jonathan, we find the thought-provoking sentence, "Jonathan loved him as his own soul" (1 Sam. 18:1). This was not meant as a criticism that Jonathan should cease loving his own soul and instead transfer all his love to David. Jonathan did love his own heart. He did not say, "I'm afraid of myself and I'm worthless." Rather Jonathan loved himself and that enabled him to have a deep friendship.

I ask myself: Do I love my own soul? Do I sometimes talk to my soul as David did in Psalm 103? "Hello, soul, listen! Can you hear me? Bless the Lord, O my soul, and forget not all his benefits."

Does all that I have discussed thus far have anything to do with marriage? It certainly does. It has everything to do with it. Everything!

In his famous passage about marriage, Ephesians 5:21-33, the Apostle Paul refers no less than three times to self-love. In verse 28 we read, "Even so husbands should love their wives as their own bodies. He who loves his wife loves himself." And verse 29 says, "For no man ever hates his own flesh, but nourishes it and cherishes it. . . ." Finally, verse 33 states, "Let each one of you love his wife as himself. . . ."

I must admit that I had preached many times about this text before this straightforward statement, which sounds so odd to our ears, really struck me: "Whoever loves his wife, loves himself." This certainly cannot mean that whoever loves his wife is egocentric. On the contrary, whoever loves his wife proves that he has acquired self-acceptance and thus has learned to love himself. It is interesting that Paul explicitly mentions the physical dimension of self-acceptance. "Even so husbands should love their wives as their own bodies. . . . For no man ever hates his own flesh. . . ."

Just as Jonathan and David's deep friendship causes me to ask myself, "Do I love my own soul?" in the same way I should ask myself, "Do I love my own body?" Do I really love myself, body and soul?

Self-love and selfishness I can well imagine that many who have followed my thoughts to this point have become quite nervous and uncomfortable. Does this not contradict what we, as good Christians, have been brought up to believe? Is it not written, "He who loves his life loses it" (Jn. 12:25). "If any one comes to me and does not hate . . . even his own life, he cannot be my disciple" (Lk. 14:26). "If any man would come after me, let him deny himself . . ." (Mt. 16:24).

Indeed we are so ingrained with the idea of self-denial, self-sacrifice and the fear of being egotistical that the admonition to love one's self seems almost a blasphemy. What then is the distinction between self-love and selfishness, between self-acceptance and egoism?

One difficulty lies in the fact that the word *self-love* has a double meaning. It can mean self-acceptance as well as self-centeredness. Along the same line, Josef Piper, in his essay "Zucht und Mass," stresses, "There are two opposing ways in which a man can love himself: selflessly or selfishly. Only the first is self-preserving, while the second is self-destroying."

An example of self-love in the negative sense is illustrated by the Greek myth about Narcissus. He was a youth who, while gazing at his reflection in a well, fell in love with himself. Totally engrossed with his own image, he tumbled into the water and drowned. From this myth, the word *narcissism* is derived. Another Greek term for "self" and "love" denoting the same idea is *auto-eroticism*.

Self-love used in the positive sense of self-acceptance is the exact opposite of narcissism or auto-eroticism. It is actually a prerequisite for a step in the direction of self-lessness. We cannot give what we do not possess. Only when we have accepted ourselves can we become truly self-less and free from ourselves. If, however, we have not found ourselves and discovered our own identity, then we must continually search for ourselves. The word *self-centered* aptly describes us when we revolve only around ourselves.

To put it bluntly, *Whoever does not love himself is an egoist.* He must become an egoist necessarily because he is not sure of his identity and is therefore always trying to find himself. Like Narcissus, being engrossed with himself, he becomes self-centered.

Hermann Hesse, in his novel *Steppenwolf,* which won the Nobel Prize for Literature in 1946, describes the intricate relationship between the lack of self-love (which he calls self-hate) and self-centeredness (which he calls "sheer egoism") or the inability to love others. He says about Harry Haller, the hero of the novel: *As for others and the world around him he never ceased in his heroic and earnest endeavour to love them, to be just to them, to do them no harm, for the love of his neighbour was as strongly forced upon him as the hatred of himself, and so his whole life was an example that the love of one's neighbour is not possible without love of oneself, and that self-hate is really the same thing as sheer egoism, and in the long run breeds the same cruel isolation and despair.*[4]

This throws light on modern man's striving to escape isolation and despair by trying to find himself. In his search, Haller employs various means such as drinking, over-eating, "tripping" and experimenting with sex. These are all expressions of a lack of self-acceptance. Those who are searching attempt to find self-fulfillment easily through drugs, alcohol, food and sex. These result, however, in a still deeper dissatisfaction and an endless striving. Modern man's perpetual search is so self-centered precisely because he neither loves nor accepts himself.

Self-acceptance excludes self-centeredness. For love "does not demand its own way" (1 Cor. 13:5, Living Bible). Love has found its own way. We can give only that which we have, lose only that which we possess and "hate" only that which we love. The word *hate* as used in Luke 14:26 is not meant in the emotional sense. It is rather the ability to free ourselves from the bondage of our own personal desires and needs. Self-love is necessary before we can be freed from ourselves.

Self-acceptance means "I love me," and it enables me to turn my attention outwards. Auto-eroticism means "I love I" and means that I am unable to look beyond myself. Self-love must be acquired. Auto-eroticism is inborn.

All of us experience the auto-erotical phase before we are five years old and again at the onset of puberty. If we remain in this self-centered phase, however, we will never acquire true self-love.

The "crush" is an emotional expression of the auto-erotical phase. The adolescent often has an idol with whom he is in love and on whom he projects his own identity. He loves the image of himself which he sees in the other person, as Narcissus loved his reflection in the well. The dream is shattered the moment the idol is viewed from a realistic stance and is no longer congruent with the adolescent's projected image.

Masturbation is a physical manifestation of the auto-erotical phase. It is an immature sexual expression coinciding with the stage of puberty and thus ought not to cause anxiety. Physically speaking, masturbation is not harmful to one's health. Nevertheless, this is not a legitimate argument which can be used to minimize the harm caused if practiced beyond this state.

Of greater concern is the effect which masturbation might have on the development of one's personality. If a person over twenty still finds it necessary to masturbate, this may be an indication that he has remained in the auto-erotical phase and has not yet acquired self-love. The development of his personality is hindered because he is trying to play simultaneously the roles of giver and taker. He who has fully accepted himself does not need to masturbate. He can "let go of himself" in every sense of the word. He is mature enough to love.

I am reminded of a couple whom all their friends would describe as very unselfish. This couple's home is open to all kinds of people in need. They are always ready to help and to serve others.

I knew them even before they knew each other. They both came from very unloving homes with strict, demanding parents, where words of praise were scarce or non-existent. As a result they both developed a poor self-image and struggled with masturbation as a sort of comfort and substitute for the lack of being loved. For the young man, masturbation became an almost daily habit.

As soon as they fell in love with each other, this habit came to an abrupt end, and they could both return from this dead end road. Not because they released their sex drives by petting or premarital intercourse, but because they opened each other's eyes to see the positive sides in one another. They helped each other to love themselves. There is no doubt in my mind that this healthy self-love which they developed was the secret of their unselfishness.

Jesus and self-acceptance The relationship between self-love and selflessness, between self-acceptance and self-denial, is best illustrated by Jesus Christ. Jesus wholly knew himself and he was completely in harmony with himself. With absolute authority he could say, "Before Abraham was, I am" (Jn. 8:58). And with the God who himself said, "I am who I am" (Ex. 3:14), Jesus declared, "I and the Father are one" (Jn. 10:30).

It is interesting to note that in the New Testament statements regarding Christ's identity precede statements concerning his self-denial. For example, before Jesus washed his disciples' feet, there is a majestic declaration of his total self-acceptance: "Jesus knew that the Father had given all things into his hands, and that he had come from God and was going to God" (Jn. 13:3).

Self-acceptance and selflessness are interrelated. Jesus knew who he was and accepted his identity and purpose. Self-acceptance was an intrinsic part of his life, enabling him to turn his attention outwards and to love truly the people with whom he came into contact. It was unnecessary for him forcefully to establish his equality with God, or to search gropingly for his own identity. Rather he "emptied himself, taking the form of a servant. . . . And being found in human form he humbled himself and became obedient unto death, even death on a cross" (Phil. 2: 7-8). Here too Jesus' self-denial is preceded by a statement of his identity: "though he was in the form of God" (Phil. 2:6). In short, since Jesus loved himself, he was selfless and able to love others "as he loved himself."

"That's easy enough for Jesus," we might say, "but who are we?" Paul deals with this objection by saying simply, "Your attitude should be the kind that was shown us by Jesus Christ" (Phil. 2:5, Living Bible).

If Jesus Christ is our life this means that the acceptance of ourselves is indeed "the foundation of all existence" as Guardini would say. Discipleship is not possible without it. The obedience of self-denial presupposes the obedience of self-acceptance.

Learning to love ourselves If it is true that self-love is the foundation of our love for others and if it is true that it is not innate but acquired, then we must face the pressing question, How can we learn to accept ourselves, to love ourselves?

Essentially, there is only one answer to this question: We must learn to let ourselves be loved. With this statement I would like to point out that it is not enough that love is offered to us. Another step is also necessary: We must learn to receive it. We must learn to accept acceptance.

The other day I observed a woman who received a compliment about a nice dress she was wearing. She shrugged the compliment off by saying, "Oh, this is just an old thing I've had hanging in my closet for years." Even if this was true—very likely it was not—it was clear to me that she had not learned the art of receiving recognition, of accepting acceptance.

The counter-example is that of a woman we know who keeps a notebook of enjoyable experiences in her life. Here she also puts down in writing compliments she has received from members of her family or friends. Just one example: One day her four-year-old told her, "You are the best Mommy in the world." Whenever she feels down or depressed, she just opens this book to lift herself up.

It seems to me that because of a misconception of Christian modesty and humility we are inclined to ward off any expressions of praise. Yes, we even tend to mistrust those who praise us and doubt the motives behind their affirmation. For this reason we discourage those who laud us until they give up expressing love to us. In this way we deprive ourselves of the experience of being loved, which is so necessary if we want to learn to love ourselves.

Martin Buber said, "Man comes to himself only via the 'you.' " Michelangelo wrote to the woman he loved, "When I am yours, then I am at last completely myself." As far as marriage is concerned, it would be entirely justified to alter Paul's statement in Ephesians 5:28 by saying, "He who is loved by his wife, learns to love himself."

The first chance we have in life to experience being loved is when we are nursed at our mother's breasts. Here

our physical and emotional needs are wholly and unconditionally met. A baby just sucks and sucks and sucks, and
no demands are made of him. Those deprived of this experience as infants may, later on in life, find it relatively
harder to build a foundation for self-love and self-acceptance.

Unfortunately breastfeeding has been on the decline
for many years, even to the extent of doctors advising
mothers against it. This could explain the increasing number of people today who seek oral satisfaction through
smoking and drinking.

The chain smoker is certainly not the "he-man" he
attempts to portray. Neither is the woman with a cigarette
hanging from her lips *e-man*-cipated. On the contrary, an
addiction to nicotine and alcohol may indicate a futile
attempt to provide a substitute for the mother's breast,
which was denied in infancy. It may express a longing for
being loved which the individual hopes will enable him to
love himself.

However, as Dr. Groeger has pointed out, to be accepted and loved is important not only in infancy and
childhood, but throughout one's life. We need it as adults
too. We all know how encouraged we are by a word of
recognition or affirmation in our daily work. No one is
able to work without it every now and then. It is as necessary as bread for our daily life—perhaps for men even
more than for women.

Why? I don't know. But it is a fact that the male ego is
weaker than the female ego. Maybe it is because the man
was at the receiving end from the very beginning—as a
suckling. Maybe it is because it is easier for women to at-

tract attention simply because they *are* more beautiful.

Recently I observed teen-agers at a summer camp. I saw how easily the girls attracted others because of their beautiful figures, hair styles and make-up. The 16-year-old boys with their pimply faces, drab jeans and T-shirts were not such a pretty sight. I felt how much these boys longed for recognition and admiration. I believe few women realize how much a man is dependent upon a woman's praise, even more than the other way around.

These differences though are relative. All of us need the "daily bread" of praise, and it is precisely this "daily bread" which we withhold from each other. We are quick to criticize and slow to praise. Often we express only negative remarks and in this way destroy the self-confidence of those around us. Church circles are no exception.

Such a negative atmosphere fosters the development of the person whom Dr. Groeger defines as one who "loves out of duty," whose love does not spring from joy but is forced or, as Hermann Hesse puts it, comes out of an "heroic and earnest endeavour."

Have we not been in this situation ourselves from time to time? We don't feel like loving, but we tell ourselves, "I should love, I should love, I should love!" It is like doing spiritual chin-ups in an effort to please others and God. But we all know how it is with chin-ups. For a limited time we can pull ourselves up, but then inevitably the moment comes when we run out of strength and have to give up. It is like a car which runs out of gas. You can push it a little way, but you won't get very far, especially not uphill.

When I was in Africa, one of my fellow missionaries

constructed a windmill. He planned to draw water out of a deep well by means of wind power. The idea was great. But when there was no wind we had no water. A man on a bicycle had to produce the power. You can guess just how long it was before he was tired.

A person who loves out of duty is like the man on the bicycle. He tries to produce love by his own effort. He receives no power from outside. He cannot love, because he is neither loved nor praised. And on the other hand, he is not loved and praised, because he does not love.

A vicious circle What I have described thus far is actually a vicious circle:

> We are unable to love others because we have not learned to love ourselves.
>
> We cannot learn to love ourselves because we are not loved by others or are unable to accept their love.
>
> We are not loved by others because we are unable to love them or we love them only "out of duty."
>
> We are unable to love them because we have not learned to love ourselves.

And so the vicious circle starts again from the beginning.

And what if no "wind from outside" ever hits us? What happens to the person who has never known what it is to be loved? What happens to the child who grows up never having experienced the warmth and security of a loving home, of parents who care and spend time with him? And if he gets only reproof and criticism at school and again at work, what then? If it is true that a man comes to himself only via the "you," what happens then to someone who has never related to a "you"?

Is such a person destined to a life of loneliness and a vain search for self-acceptance? Is there no power able to break this vicious circle?

The breakthrough from outside Psychologists and philosophers can ably describe and explain this vicious circle, but they cannot help us to break it. It cannot be broken from inside. There must be an outside source.

In Romans 15:7, the Apostle Paul points to this outside source: "Accept one another, therefore, *as Christ has accepted us* for the glory of God" (NEB).

Jesus Christ is the power from outside breaking the vicious circle. Now we get ground under our feet. Jesus Christ is the only one who accepts us as we are, fully, unconditionally, and therefore he makes it possible for us to accept ourselves as well as one another.

Take baptism as an example. There are certainly many weighty and justified questions which can be asked concerning the practice of infant baptism. This message, however, is conveyed clearly through it: God has accepted me unconditionally before I could do anything to earn his love.

Martin Luther, who was deprived of warmth and love as a child, wrestled his whole life long with self-acceptance. To help himself when in the throes of deep doubts, he scrawled in large print on his desk, "I have been baptized."

Through Christ, God has taken the initiative in love. He spoke the first word. He took the first step. Therefore we can love: "We love, because he first loved us" (1 Jn. 4:19).

The question is, How much does this fact mean to me

personally? Does it mean enough so that I can stop blaming my childhood or my past circumstances or other people for my inability to love? Can I stop sitting on the pity pot and allow God's love to transform me?

The parents of a distinguished family phoned us. Their son was hospitalized after an unsuccessful suicide attempt.

"I am going to do it again" was the first thing he told us when my wife and I visited him.

"Why?"

"I am an error, a mistake. I am not supposed to exist."

We did not understand.

Slowly the full story emerged. He had overheard a nasty conversation of his parents and learned that he was an unwanted child. His mother had forgotten to take the pill, and in anger his father had reminded her of it and blamed her for it.

This experience had crushed him. What was the meaning, the purpose, of his life, if he was not supposed to live in the first place? If his parents did not want him, who did?

God? Does God want all children to be born who are born? Even if their parents did not want them to be born? These questions had been too hard for him. So he had rung the alarm bell.

"God wants you," we assured him.

"How do you know?" He looked at us with eyes that expressed doubt and hope at the same time.

"God was himself an unwanted child," I answered, "an embarrassment to his parents, unexpected and unplanned. No human action was involved in his coming into being—let alone a human desire. Actually he remained an unwanted person all his life—until they tried to kick him out of this world by crucifying him."

"And still," my wife added, "there has never been a child more wanted, more loved by God and never a person who became a greater blessing to more people than Jesus."

The face of the boy expressed unbelieving amazement.

"I—a blessing?"

"Yes, a special blessing," we confirmed him.

Never had we understood in a deeper way the invasion of God into the vicious circle. The totally unaccepted one accepts the totally unaccepted. The unwanted God wants those who are unwanted. The unloved God loves those who are unloved. The Incarnation defines the true humanity of man. Therefore there is acceptance for everyone.

We prayed together with the boy and witnessed his acceptance of God's acceptance.

Love is more than acceptance. So far I have used the words *love* and *acceptance* interchangeably. But here it should be added that love is more than mere acceptance.

Christ accepts us as we are: "Him who comes to me I will not cast out" (Jn. 6:37). But when he accepts us, we cannot remain as we are. Acceptance is nothing but the first step of love. Then it exposes us to a process of growth. Being accepted by the love of Christ means being transformed.

In his fourth thesis which he nailed on the church door in Wittenberg, Luther stated, "God's love does not love that which is worthy of being loved, but it creates that which is worthy of being loved." God's love does not allow us to remain as we are. It is more than mere acceptance.

It works and forms, it carves out the image which God has intended. This is a life-long process and sometimes a painful one since growth is connected with pain. God says, "I accept you as you are, but now the work of love begins. I need your cooperation—your self-love."

Someone asked me in confusion, "Is this not a contradiction? On one hand I should accept myself as I am—'agree to be the person who I am.' On the other hand I should work on myself and change and grow?"

My answer: God's love does not exempt us from the obligation of working on ourselves, but it makes this work possible, promising and hopeful. To let God accept me and to accept myself does not mean to sit back passively and say, "This is just the way I am—I can't do anything about it." It means rather to allow God's chisel of love to work on me. Self-acceptance is merely the necessary first step in a process of growth.

Dr. Theodor Bovet writes, "If I love myself in the right way, then it is impossible for me to remain standing still. On the contrary, I want to change so that I can become that which God desires me to become. In the same way we should love also our neighbor."[5]

Some readers have reacted critically to my book *I Loved a Girl,* saying that I did not accept François, the young man with whom I was corresponding, because I tried to change him. Actually, I did accept him, as the first letters show. But then I challenged him to change his ways precisely because I loved him. Love is more than acceptance. We want to see our neighbor become all that God created him to be.

2 The Consequences of the Lack of Self-Love

If we love ourselves in the wrong way, then it is impossible to grow and develop into the people God wants us to be. Many problems result from the lack of self-love. I have already discussed the search for self-identity through drinking, eating, "tripping" and experimenting with sex. But other problems too can result from the lack of self-love.

The auto-erotical choice of profession and partner The choice of entering into people-oriented professions may be motivated by the need to be needed. It often stems from an unconscious attempt to make up for a deficiency of love. By placing himself in a position where he is needed by others, the unloved person attempts to fulfill his own needs and bolster his own self-concept.

However, as Dr. Groeger points out, this is a miscalculation. Such a helper cannot really help, for he needs the needy one more than the needy one needs him. He may need him to such a degree that the more he tries to help the more he becomes entangled with himself and is therefore unable to really understand the other one.

The choice of a life partner can also be an attempt to make up for a deficiency of love. Such a choice will always result in a very difficult marriage. He who cannot love himself will confront his spouse with insatiable demands and long for the love of the other one without being either able or willing to give something in return. Cruel as it may sound, marriage is no sanatorium for love-cripples. A deficiency of self-love cannot be restored just by getting married.

Hostility toward the body If I am unable to accept myself, I am unable to accept my body. Hostility toward the body is always a symptom of lack of self-love. He who does not love himself does not love his body either.

In his book *A Place for You*, Dr. Paul Tournier gives two examples of such a negative attitude toward the body. They remind me of our experience with the Scandinavian student related at the beginning of this book:

A pretty woman confides in me that her first act when she goes into a hotel bedroom is to turn all mirrors with their faces to the wall. Another tells me that she has never been able to look at herself naked without a feeling of shame. "This body of mine," she adds, "is my enemy."[6]

These women were unable to accept their own bodies because they were unable to accept themselves.

Such hatred for one's body will, of course, have a negative effect on marriage. As I have already mentioned, the Apostle Paul in Ephesians 5 specifically emphasizes the physical dimension of self-acceptance. Marriage problems in the sexual realm are usually connected with the fact that at least one of the partners has difficulty in accepting his body.

Could that be the reason why so many Christians fail to achieve sexual harmony in marriage? Many Christians seem to have the feeling that their physical relationship, if not "worldly" or even sinful, is somehow less good in God's eyes than their spiritual fellowship, that the body is less pleasing to God than the soul. It is not surprising that such an unhealthy attitude toward the body affects their physical harmony.

You will find in circles where the sinfulness of man is constantly stressed, and as a consequence healthy self-love is downgraded as sinful pride, that a deep-seated disrespect or even hatred of the body is the result. It is hard to imagine adherents of such a theology ever joining a gymnastic club, let alone taking dancing lessons, though this could be a decisive help in developing a positive self-image of the body and overcoming this particular neurosis.

As Dr. Tournier writes,
Gymnastics, especially the dance, singing, and all the arts of bodily self-expression, have great therapeutic value. It is not a matter of accepting willy-nilly that one has a body, but of rediscovering its value, of using it as a genuine manifestation of one's person, and of becoming aware once more of its spiritual significance. The body is the

place of love. The sex act is not merely the expression of one's feelings, but the sublime gift of oneself, a true spiritual testament.[7]

An additional aid for the woman, single or married, who wishes to learn to love her body and herself is to live consciously in harmony with her menstrual cycle. The cycle is as unique and individual as one's fingerprint. This is why the intimate knowledge of its individual characteristics can help a woman tremendously in finding her own identity.[8]

Abortion and hostility toward children When we travel from country to country we are struck by the increasing hostility toward children throughout the world. Interestingly this is not so prevalent in some of the countries behind the Iron Curtain, let alone in the Third World, but especially in the so-called Christian West.

I remember when we came from Africa to Germany with five children of kindergarten and grade school age, it was next to impossible for us to find a place to live, for the children a place to play, and for all of us a place where we could spend our vacations together. In Finland we met young couples with two children who would like to have had a third child (and there is certainly no over-population in Finland!), but they were afraid of being ostracized by society. In America too we have met mothers who were ashamed because they had become pregnant a third time.

It seems to me that there is a direct relationship between the lack of self-acceptance, the hostility toward the body and the hostility toward children. Bringing forth children is a part of the physical dimension of life. He who does not have a positive relationship to his body will find it difficult to reach a positive relationship to the child, who is a fruit of his body.

I wonder whether one of the deepest roots of the abortion problem does not lie here. Could it be that this also is the result of non-self-acceptance which expresses itself in a hostile act against the unborn fruit of the body? Can an expectant mother who wishes to abort her child really love herself? Otherwise how could she act so egotistically?

Over-eating and under-eating It is strange, but it seems to me that while a man requires relatively more personal recognition, a woman finds it relatively more difficult to develop a positive relationship to her own body. In our many interviews with women who possess a poor self-image, my wife and I have discovered two symptoms which occur repeatedly: Either these women eat too much or they eat too little. Both over-eating and under-nourishing one's self are expressions of the same disease—lack of self-love.

Through the lack of self-love an empty hole is created. Over-eating—or getting drunk—is the futile attempt to fill up this empty hole. On the other hand, under-eating, denying the body what it needs, may cover up an attempt to punish and deny the unloved self. Yes, it may be a way of saying, "I'd like to get rid of myself, be free of myself."

But true freedom of one's self, true "self-lessness" cannot be achieved so cheaply. It can only be accomplished through the longer and more costly process of learning self-acceptance.

The ultimate expression of the wish to be free of one's self, by-passing the route of self-acceptance, is suicide. Suicide is the ultimate expression of hostility toward the body and of non-self-acceptance.

Fear Whoever takes this final drastic step and attempts suicide demonstrates that he fears life more than death. Fear too is a result of a lack of self-love.

"Love seeketh not her own," writes Paul in 1 Corinthians 13:5 (AV). But he who does not know what love is and cannot love himself must always "seek" himself, constantly pursued by the fear that perhaps he will never discover that for which he is searching. Consequently, the self-centered person tends to be apprehensive. He revolves around his own axis, losing sight of all else but himself and his own interests. In such a person, fear takes root. The egoist feels insecure, unprotected and at the mercy of a cruel, unloving world. He clings to himself defensively, afraid that to do otherwise would ensure personal defeat and destruction.

Precisely because fear and self-centeredness are so closely bound together, we are susceptible to a specific variety of fear which is especially widespread today, namely the fear of failure. It is a natural by-product of modern man's idolatry of accomplishment. From early childhood we are indoctrinated with the philosophy that performance determines worth. When a machine ceases to be productive, it is discarded. Likewise if a person fails to perform at the level expected of him, he is considered useless. Our society has no room for "failures" and so non-achievers become ostracized.

An outcast, however, cannot love himself. He whom society judges worthless cannot acquire the feeling of self-respect and self-worth which a person needs in order to be able to live. Therefore, the fear of failure becomes greater than the fear of death.

Once more we encounter the connection between lack of self-love and of suicide. The potential suicide feels trapped between his fear of failure and his own self-centeredness. Thus he concludes that the only way to get rid of his fear is to get rid of himself.

But suicide is not the answer. The answer is to learn how to live with fear.

In this respect a word of Jesus has become very helpful to me: "In the world you have tribulation; but be of good cheer, I have overcome the world" (Jn. 16:33). The Greek word for "tribulation" conveys precisely the idea of "being pressured," "being trapped." The German translation uses the word *Angst*. It is the same word we find in "anxiety" and "anguish." It comes from *Enge* and means "strait," "narrowness," being in a tight spot, in a bottleneck, zeroed in. All these expressions describe ably the experience of fear.

For me the greatest help of this verse is that it ends the myth that as a Christian I have to be fearless. Jesus states it soberly, realistically, matter-of-factly: "In the world you have such tribulation. In the world you have fear."

The first help in learning how to handle fear is to stop fighting it. My own experience during the Second World War was a tremendous school in learning how to live with fear. Sometimes I had to live for days and weeks in the fear of being killed any minute, almost any second.

Every time the roar of the Russian artillery was heard, I knew that within the next few seconds it would be decided whether I would live or die. It was an uninterrupted exercise of living with fear.

I remember that the first help for me was that I stopped fighting fear and learned to admit to myself, "Walter, you are afraid." In that moment the tight grip of fear loosened, and fear became bearable. Yes, it even became a positive force challenging my faith.

Faith did not free me from fear, but fear forced me to believe. Every time I heard the roar of the enemy fire, I threw myself down into the ditch or foxhole where I was. In an act of surrender to the One who has overcome the world, I said, "You have me completely." I can only express it in a paradoxical way: I learned not to be afraid of fear.

At this point it is important to notice that Jesus did not say, "I have overcome tribulation. I have overcome fear." But, "I have overcome the world." This gives us another decisive help in dealing with fear. We cannot attack fear directly, but only indirectly according to the rule of the "Knight's move" in chess. The Knight is not allowed to attack his opponent straight-on, but only "around the corner." In the same way we can only deal with fear "around the corner" in an act of surrender to the One who has overcome the world—including our own merciless, achievement-oriented society.

Herein lies our hope and consolation: This One who overcame the world had fear himself. He lived through such agonies that "his sweat became like great drops of blood" (Lk. 22:44). Through the power of his fears Christ gives us strength to live with fear, not to be afraid of it, yes, to "cheer up" in the midst of fear and tribulation. "Cheer up, for I have overcome the world" (Jn. 16:33, Living Bible). In Christ we can cheerfully have fear.

With the word *cheerful*, however, I touch another sore spot. Maybe the lack of cheerfulness is the most common manifestation of the lack of self-love found today. Therefore the final part of this book shall be dedicated to this problem.

3 Depression & Helps in Overcoming It

Depression too in the final analysis is, I believe, a result of the lack of self-love.

It is astounding how many depressed people there are. It is still more astounding how many depressed Christians there are. I am not speaking here of superficial Christians who lack vital faith and spiritual depth. No, I am thinking of many sincere believers who live in a personal relationship to Jesus Christ and who in spite of it have to struggle again and again with deep depressions.

At the root of every depression is the feeling of having lost something. Outward circumstances can be the cause: the loss of material goods, the loss of health, the loss of a beloved one, the loss of confidence, the loss of self-respect in becoming guilty, the loss of an ability perhaps as a result of aging. We react to these experiences of loss with sadness, self-pity, mourning, disappointment, envy, shame and self-depreciation. All these feelings flow together like little brooks in the stream of a general feeling of depression.

Today especially three kinds of depression are on the increase. First, there is a depression stemming from exhaustion. Especially executives, top-achievers and over-conscientious housewives suffer from it. They experience the loss of being able to achieve perfection. Their feeling of self-competence and "the sky's the limit" slowly fades away and throws them into depression out of complete exhaustion.

Another specific depression is induced by moving to a different residence. Even rearranging furniture and redecorating can result in a feeling of loss. One feels uprooted and is acutely aware that one's home, the four walls one knew so well, are missing.

There is even a depression stemming from the loss of a task or of a certain burden we have to carry. Depression stemming from retirement is one version of it. Strangely enough it strikes not so long as we are burdened by a certain task, but in the moment the burden is lifted. When the job has been completed, when the battle has been won, when the exam has been passed, when the tension has been relieved and the conflict solved—then this kind of depression hits us out of the blue sky. The loss of a challenge, of work or of a struggle precipitates us into an aching void.

There is also a depression stemming from no apparent outside cause, but which assails a person from within. It can manifest itself in either restless, nervous energy or passive inertia, which make any constructive action impossible. Such a "depression from inside" is usually accompanied by tormenting self-accusations and exaggerated guilt feelings. Although no tangible source can be found, ideas of being deprived, poor, small and inferior persist and lead to a complete loss of any feeling of self-worth.

This explains why the depressed person is so vulnerable and oversensitive when confronted with criticism. He cleaves and clings to other people and longs desperately for recognition and the assurance of being loved, in order to be able to love himself.

The deepest root of depression is the feeling that I have lost myself and have given up hope of ever finding myself again. There is nothing in me worth loving. I grope into a void when I try to love myself.

This means that self-acceptance and depression are closely interrelated. The above description of various forms of depression vividly depicts a self-centeredness which we recognize as a natural consequence of a lack of self-love. Therefore, the best protection against depression is for us to learn to love ourselves, and at the same time victory over depression enables us to acquire self-acceptance.

Depression in the Bible In overcoming depression, it is encouraging to know that the Bible, that tremendously human book, understands us with these feelings.

There is the well-known story of King Saul who was often plagued by deep depression and depended upon

David, the shepherd boy, to help soothe him by playing on his lyre: "Now the Spirit of the LORD departed from Saul, and an evil spirit from the LORD tormented him. . . . Whenever the evil spirit from God was upon Saul, David took the lyre and played it with his hand; so Saul was refreshed, and was well, and the evil spirit departed from him" (1 Sam. 16:14, 23).

From this story, we can gain a helpful hint in counteracting depression. Music conveys harmony and order and thus can heal a mind in disorder and disharmony.

The Bible offers us another example in the story of Nebuchadnezzar. Having disregarded a dream sent by God to warn him against illusions of grandeur and to admonish him to repent, Nebuchadnezzar fell into a deep depression and lived as a wild animal: "He was driven from among men, and ate grass like an ox, and his body was wet with the dew of heaven till his hair grew as long as eagles' feathers, and his nails were like birds' claws" (Dan. 4:33).

Nebuchadnezzar, however, relates how he overcame this depression and gives us another helpful hint—namely the act of praise and thanksgiving: "At the end of the days I, Nebuchadnezzar, lifted my eyes to heaven, and my reason returned to me, and I blessed the Most High, and praised and honored him who lives for ever" (Dan. 4:34).

Another example from the Old Testament is the story about Elijah in 1 Kings 19. Interestingly enough depression struck him after a spiritual highlight experience, after a great battle of the Lord had been won. In a state of great physical exhaustion, he "sat down under a broom tree; and he asked that he might die, saying: 'It is enough; O

LORD, take away my life; for I am no better than my fathers' " (1 Kings 19:4).

Again we can learn a lot from the way the Lord dealt with his depression. No reprimand, no appeal to the will, but instead loving care, rest, food—and touch: "And he lay down and slept under a broom tree; and behold, an angel touched him, and said to him, 'Arise and eat.' And he looked, and behold, there was at his head a cake baked on hot stones and a jar of water. And he ate and drank, and lay down again" (v. 5).

In the New Testament, the outstanding figure is the Apostle Paul. He was certainly, by nature, subject to depressions. Romano Guardini in his book *The Image of Jesus in the New Testament* vividly portrays this side of the apostle. Through his description, I must say, Paul became more human to me. Guardini writes about Paul, "He seemed to be a man who attracted that which was difficult, against whom fate seemed to be pitted, a harassed man. . . . He had to suffer much, continuously and in all situations."

Paul was a rabbinical student, a discipline which served to nurture his perfectionistic tendencies. The same depression which assails all top-achievers when they are faced with the reality of their own human limitations and failings is certainly contained at least in the undertones of the following sentences: "I do not understand my own actions. For I do not do what I want, but I do the very thing I hate. . . . For I know that nothing good dwells within me, that is, in my flesh. I can will what is right, but I cannot do it. For I do not do the good I want, but the evil I do not want is what I do" (Rom. 7:15, 18-19).

One cannot help but ask the question: What evil might this man have done to cause him to talk like this? Walter Uhsadel, professor of theology at Tübingen University, comments on this: "The inner vulnerability of depressed persons causes them to be more aware of their failings and to suffer more under the burden of this knowledge than other people."[9]

Focusing on the last few chapters of 2 Corinthians, Uhsadel points out another typical symptom of a depressed person which Paul demonstrates as he vacillates between boasting and self-devaluation. Simultaneously, we can sense Paul's deep longing for recognition, appreciation and love as expressed in 2 Corinthians 12:11: "I have been a fool! You forced me to it, for I ought to have been commended by you. For I am not at all inferior to these superlative apostles, even though I am nothing."

I am aware that one must be careful not to "psychologize" Scripture. But I believe it was precisely Paul's sensitive nature which God used to clarify man's character and his relationship to God.

The book of the Bible, however, where I feel most understood is the Psalms. The one who prayed Psalm 31, for instance, certainly knew what depression was:

Be gracious to me, O LORD, for I am in distress;
my eye is wasted from grief,
my soul and my body also.
For my life is spent with sorrow,
and my years with sighing;
my strength fails because of my misery,
and my bones waste away. (vv. 9-10).

This feeling: I am spent, consumed, "eaten up." I am

becoming less and less; I am vanishing away. Time crawls slowly along without an end or purpose. We can visualize them—this crowd of sighing Christians.

What psychosomatic medicine has discovered today the psalmist experienced long ago. Body and soul are a unity. Grief of the soul means grief of the body. The psalmist's depression assaults even his bones.

I am the scorn of all my adversaries,
a horror to my neighbors,
an object of dread to my acquaintances;
those who see me in the street flee from me. . . .
Yea, I hear the whispering of many—
terror on every side!—
as they scheme together against me,
as they plot to take my life. (vv. 11,13)

This feeling: I am threatened, trapped. I have only enemies. Everyone is against me; nobody understands me. Nobody accepts me. Nobody loves me. I have no more strength to defend myself, no more ambition to seek friendship. I am hopelessly alone.

I have passed out of mind like one who is dead;
I have become like a broken vessel. (v. 12)

This feeling: I cannot contain myself, hold myself together. I am being poured out; everything is flowing out of me and I am losing, losing, losing.

Helps in overcoming depression The Bible clearly shows that God realizes we have these feelings and that he understands us when we do. Maybe from this fact we can derive already a help in dealing with depressions: We do not need to be ashamed of them. They are no flaw in our make-up or a discredit to the name "Christian."

On the other hand, however, we should not sit on the pity pot and mope the whole day. At one time when my wife was rather depressed, she asked one of our teenage sons, "What shall I do?" After a few minutes' reflection, he answered, "Above all, Mommy, do something! Don't just do nothing!" It was precisely the right word for her at that moment.

In a way each person is his own best doctor when it comes to curing depression. I know a lady who often suffers from depression with no apparent outward cause. When she is in this state it prohibits her from thinking clearly and acting objectively, so she has made for herself what she calls a "depression emergency kit." Like a doctor's prescription, she has written down instructions to herself telling her what to do in case of a depression. First of all, she has a little box of cards with special Bible verses containing promises and assurance. She picks out a card and reads it aloud. Next, she makes herself a good cup of tea which she sips slowly while listening to a favorite record. She also has on hand an absorbing book which she has been burning to read but which she has saved for this occasion. Afterward she calls up a friend and combines the visit to her with a walk in the fresh air.

Do we sense that we must have at least a bit of self-love if we would choose this method of attacking depression?

I mentioned already the unhappy childhood and strict religious upbringing which caused Martin Luther great difficulties in learning to love himself. To love himself meant for him only the sinful streak in man tending toward egoism. From what we have learned thus far concerning the interaction between the lack of self-love and depression, it is no wonder that Martin Luther was a man sorely afflicted by depression. Precisely because of his own experiences he is able to give us sound advice. I would like to share some of his suggestions with you, adding comments of my own:[10]

1. *Avoid being alone.* Luther states that isolation is poison for the depressed person, for through this the devil attempts to keep him in his power. "Talk among yourselves, so that I know I am surrounded by people," requested Luther in one of his "table talks." It was supposedly at a moment when he felt himself down.

2. *Seek out people or situations which generate joy.* Joy is always pleasing to God, even though it may not always be of a religious origin. Enjoying a good play or movie is just as legitimate as taking a long walk in the woods.

3. *Sing and make music.* Here Luther emphasizes the active involvement necessary for a person to make music of his own rather than simply listening to it. He once advised an aristocrat who was despondent, "When you are sad and feeling discouraged, just tell yourself, 'Up! up! I must play a song on the organ in praise of my Lord.' For the Scriptures assure us that God delights in song and playing musical instruments. So play upon the keys and give yourself to song until the gloomy thoughts are passed, just as David did. If the devil continues to pester you, reprimand him saying, 'Be gone, Satan, I have to sing and play now for my Lord Jesus.' " Again, Luther refers not only to religious music here but to music in general. God is really the listener, and we give him joy by our playing, a joy that returns to lighten our own heavy hearts.

4. *Dismiss heavy thoughts.* Luther warns us of the danger of becoming engrossed by gloomy or despairing thoughts which tend to keep us awake at night or assail us the first thing in the morning. He advises us either to laugh at the devil or to scorn him, but by no means to give in to him on this matter: "But the very best thing would be to refuse to fight with the devil. Despise the depressive thoughts! Act as if you would not feel them! Think of something else and say: 'All right, devil, don't bother me. I have no time now to occupy myself with your thoughts. I must ride horseback, go places, eat, drink and do this or that. Now I must be cheerful. Come again some other day.' "[11]

5. *Rely upon the promises of Scripture.* They encourage our mind to think positively, just as the lady with the depression emergency kit realized. Especially helpful are the verses known by heart because they have helped us in a specific situation. They are like rods and staffs comforting us when walking through the valley of the shadow of death, to put it in the words of Psalm 23.

6. *Seek consolation from others.* In a state of depression, we often make a mountain out of a molehill. A friend, however, sees things in the right perspective and recognizes the positive side to which we are momentarily blind. Just as it is impossible to lift ourselves out of a swamp by grasping our own hair, in the same way we need the assistance of others to rescue us from the grip of despair. We should ask ourselves, in turn, are we the sort of people who are able to offer help to others just as God sent help to Elijah—touch, in the form of a warm assuring embrace, a good meal, rest in a quiet, orderly room. Yes, even a bouquet of flowers can put away a depression.

7. *Praise and thanksgiving.* These are powerful weapons against depression. We are reminded again of Nebuchadnezzar, who, when he raised his eyes to heaven and praised God, overcame the depression which had seized him. It helps to make a list of the things one is thankful for and then praise God for them audibly.

8. *Think of other depressed people.* This is rather a surprising suggestion from Luther, but it makes sense to me. It shakes the person out of his self-centered sorrow in which he maintains that no one else in the world has suffered as much as he.

9. *Exercise patience with yourself.* The word *exercise* is important here and can also suggest the idea of practicing or training. Sometimes we must resign ourselves to the fact that life contains valleys and deserts that simply must be endured. Just as any other skill has to be learned, we must learn how to persevere during such times of personal stress.[12] I would like to add a suggestion from my own experience. Physical exercises of any form—jogging, swimming, dancing or gardening— are all excellent devices for practicing patience with yourself. Any sweat-producing activity (and the sauna should certainly not be forgotten) that enables the entire skin surface to "weep" results in an amazingly quick recovery from depression.

10. *Believe in the blessing of depression.* There can also be a positive, fruitful side to depression. This final suggestion of Luther contains an important insight which I would like to discuss in conclusion.

The gift of depression The German word for depression is *Schwermut. Schwer* can mean "heavy" as well as "difficult." *Mut* is the word for "courage." So the word *Schwermut* contains a positive message. It means the courage to be heavy-hearted, the courage to live with what is difficult.

There is a courage involved in being depressed. There is such a thing as the gift of depression—a gift which enables us to be "heavy," to live with what is difficult. Once I heard an experienced psychiatrist say, "All people of worth and value have depressions." Indeed, shallow, superficial people seldom have depressions. It requires a certain inner substance and depth of mind to be depressed. Young children, whose mental and emotional development have not yet reached this stage, cannot experience actual depression.

Suicide can be an indication of a person's inability to be depressed.[13] It may be much easier for those lacking depth in their personality to cut the thread of life. In reference to this fact, the philosopher Landsberg made a comment which becomes increasingly meaningful the more one contemplates it: "Often a man kills himself because he is unable to despair." Suicide appears here to be a result of the inability to know true despair and endure depression. The suicide lacks the courage to be depressed. Luther's surprising suggestion, "Believe in the blessing of depression," belongs in this context.

It seems to me that creative people such as artists and musicians tend to be more susceptible to depressions, perhaps because this "courage to be heavy" is a prerequisite for fruitfulness. It is no coincidence that the poet Rainer Maria Rilke, who searched for the secret of creativity with a passion exceeding that of his contemporaries, writes in a letter from Rome in May 1904:

We know little, but that we must hold to what is difficult is a certainty that will not forsake us; it is good to be solitary, for solitude is difficult; that something is difficult must be a reason the more for us to do it.[14]

Note that Rilke associates the acceptance of what is difficult with the acceptance of solitude.

In another letter of August 12th of the same year, Rilke points out that depression—just like self-love—in working upon us transforms us and produces change. When we read his lines we are again reminded of Luther's advice to have patience with ourselves:

So you must not be frightened if a sadness rises up before you larger than any you have ever seen; if a restiveness, like light and cloud-shadows, passes over your hands and over all you do. You must think that something is happening with you, that life has not forgotten you, that it holds you in its hand; it will not let you fall. Why do you want to shut out of your life any agitation, any pain, any melancholy, since you really do not know what these states are working upon you? Why do you want to persecute yourself with the question whence all this may be coming and whither it is bound since you know that you are in the midst of transitions and wished for nothing so much as to change? If there is anything morbid in your processes, just remember that sickness is the means by which an organism frees itself of foreign matter; so one must just help it to be sick, to have its whole sickness and break out with it, for that is its progress. In you, dear sir, so much is now happening; you must be patient as a sick man and confident as a convalescent; for perhaps you are both.[15]

The poet Owlglass reports the following conversation between two friends, one of whom was suffering from a deep depression. The first asks, "Why are you so depressed, my friend?" The other one replies, "I wish I could fly away and leave all my burdens behind me. I am so full of them and so heavy-hearted because of them. Why can't I be light-hearted?" His wise friend responds with the counter-question, "Why are you not empty-hearted?"

Given the choice, which would we rather be—light-hearted and empty or heavy-hearted and full? I believe it is possible to love ourselves with a full heart, even if it is heavy, while hardly could we love ourselves with an empty heart.

Some readers certainly must have been puzzled when I dealt with the depression of King Saul. Here the Bible uses a very strange expression. It describes depression as an "evil spirit from God" (1 Sam. 16:23). An evil spirit from God?

Yes, this is authentic biblical thinking: Depression can be a part of God's plan. In the story of Saul, depression was an instrument which God used to bring David into the king's palace. To believe in the blessing of depression means to recognize that God uses even depression to fulfill his plans.

No doubt there is a God-related depression, a "godly grief," as the Apostle Paul calls it, because it "produces repentance that leads to salvation and brings no regret" (2 Cor. 7:10). Or as the Living Bible translates this passage, "For God sometimes uses sorrow in our lives to help us turn away from sin and seek eternal life."

However, such a "turn" as a fruit of depression does not happen by itself. It needs the work of faith to consciously relate depression to God and receive it out of his hands. Otherwise such a turn may not take place and depression becomes a "worldly grief producing death" (2 Cor. 7:10).

This is what actually happened to Saul. He did not succeed in relating the evil spirit to God and change his life, but he became more and more entangled in his depressive moods, until finally even music did not help him any more and he brought David into danger: "And on the morrow an evil spirit from God rushed upon Saul, and he raved within his house, while David was playing the lyre, as he did day by day. Saul had his spear in his hand; and Saul cast the spear, for he thought, 'I will pin David to the wall' " (1 Sam. 18:10-11). Depression can lead to sin when we do not relate it to God. It can become "worldly grief" producing death.

The counterpart to Saul is the depression of Jesus in the garden of Gethsemane, when he told his disciples, "My soul is very sorrowful, even to death" (Mt. 26:38). But in his prayer he succeeded in relating his depression to God and in opening himself to resources which did not come from himself: " 'Father, if thou art willing, remove this cup from me; nevertheless not my will, but thine, be done.' And there appeared to him an angel from heaven, strengthening him" (Lk. 22:42-43).

There is a depression in the midst of which we encounter God, in which we are held by God. This experience gives us the courage to love ourselves *with* our depressions and be cheerful even with a heavy heart. It reflects a depth of faith which the Apostle Paul expressed with the paradoxical statement: "As servants of God we commend ourselves in every way: . . . as *sorrowful, yet always rejoicing*" (2 Cor. 6:4, 10).

I wish so much that the girl whom I mentioned in the beginning and who could not believe and accept that she was beautiful, would read this book. Maybe it would help her to work on herself and undergo the painful-joyful learning process of self-love.

On that day when my wife and I talked with her we had too little time to do more than get her started. However, we did not let her go without taking action: We laid our hands on her and blessed her in Christ's name.

In our ministry we have experienced again and again the effectiveness of this action in the counseling process. For only Christ-centered counseling is really client-centered counseling.

We do not know where this beautiful girl is now. But we remember the words which were given to us for her. They were the same as the ones quoted above by the Apostle Paul. We blessed her that she might prove herself a servant of God—sorrowful, but always rejoicing.

Notes

[1] Dr. Guido Groeger, unpublished letter, 1967.

[2] Romano Guardini, *Die Annahme seiner selbst*, 5th ed. (Werkbandverlag: Wurzburg, 1969), pp. 14, 16.

[3] Compare the exegesis of Leviticus 19:18 by Martin Noth in *Das Alte Testament Deutsch* (Göttingen: Vandenhoek and Ruprecht, 1962), p. 122.

[4] Hermann Hesse, *Steppenwolf* (New York: Holt, Rinehart and Winston, 1961), p. 10.

[5] Theodor Bovet, *Die Liebe ist in unserer Mitte* (Tübingen: Katzmann Verlag), p. 177.

[6] Paul Tournier, *A Place for You* (New York: Harper and Row, 1968), p. 66.

[7] Ibid., p. 67.

[8] See chapter 3, "Living in Harmony with the Cycle and Fertility," of Ingrid Trobisch, *The Joy of Being a Woman and What a Man Can Do* (New York: Harper and Row, 1975), pp. 33-63.

[9] Walter Uhsadel, "Der depressive Mensch in theologischer Sicht," *Wege zum Menschen* (August 1966), p. 313.

[10] Quoted according to August Hardeland, *Geschichte der Speciellen Seelsorge* (Germany, 1893).

[11] Letter of November 22, 1532, to Johannes von Stockhausen.

[12] See Walter Trobisch, *Spiritual Dryness* (Downers Grove: InterVarsity Press, 1970).

[13] See Klages in *Wege zum Menschen*, op. cit., p. 226.

[14] Rainer Maria Rilke, *Letters to a Young Poet* (New York: W. W. Norton, 1954), p. 53.

[15] Ibid., pp. 69-70.